Balloon Wishes & Ice Cream Dreams

by
Mindy Barrientos

tate publishing
CHILDREN'S DIVISION

Published by Tate Publishing & Enterprises, LLC
127 E. Trade Center Terrace | Mustang, Oklahoma 73064 USA
1.888.361.9473 | www.tatepublishing.com

Tate Publishing is committed to excellence in the publishing industry. The company reflects the philosophy established by the founders, based on Psalm 68:11,
"The Lord gave the word and great was the company of those who published it."

Book design copyright © 2016 by Tate Publishing, LLC. All rights reserved.
Cover and interior design by James Jabonero
Illustrations by Marivir Lynn Lomocso

Published in the United States of America

ISBN: 978-1-68270-614-5
1. Juvenile Nonfiction / General
2. Juvenile Nonfiction / Family / Parents
16.04.18

This book is dedicated to the girl who stole my heart and has never let go. The girl who has caused me to expand my shores beyond what I ever knew possible and experience life through the immeasurable scope and privilege of being a mom, aka Mumzie. She is my love and joy and a blessing from God. My beautiful girl, Madeline. I love you forever and ever and ever.

~ Mom

If I could wish a hundred thousand wishes and dream a million dreams and with each wish give you a balloon and each dream a scoop of ice cream...

You would have a hundred thousand balloons—thousands of each color, no doubt—and dreams that only love could sustain, dreamt for a lifetime throughout.

There would be big balloons and small ones filled with love and happiness galore. There would be pink and red shiny ones too. And ice cream? There would be even more!

My very first wish would be for golden balloons for Jesus Christ to be your Lord and Savior forever and that He be the one to light every step of your path and be the center of your every endeavor.

Then I would dream of your
happiness. That your days would
be fun filled and true. And that
is just the beginning of an ice
cream sundae dreamed up just for
beautiful you.

Then I would wish ten thousand wishes for you to be healthy, beautiful, and bright. My love, my angel, may you use each of your gifts for goodness and doing right.

I would dream for God to give you knowledge and wisdom—both together. You see, the two go hand in hand, my love. Wisdom is the application of knowledge used fruitfully.

I dream of you with a beautiful family, putting them first in all you do. And that you are blessed with unconditional love and happiness for all your years through.

I wish for you to have endless sunny summer days that seem to never end—roller skating, swimming, lemonade stands, and slumber parties with your very best friend.

I wish for you many starry nights with dimly moonlit skies, making wishes on falling stars as you watch the moon drift quietly by.

I would wish thousands of wishes just for you to be blessed with a daughter like you of your own. You have taught me so much about how to love and about life blessings that I could not have ever known.

One day, my love, my angel, your balloons will lift you and you will fly with confidence and grace. And I pray that you will know it is love, and ice cream, that sustains you with each and every passing day.

e|LIVE

listen|imagine|view|experience

AUDIO BOOK DOWNLOAD INCLUDED WITH THIS BOOK!

In your hands you hold a complete digital entertainment package. In addition to the paper version, you receive a free download of the audio version of this book. Simply use the code listed below when visiting our website. Once downloaded to your computer, you can listen to the book through your computer's speakers, burn it to an audio CD or save the file to your portable music device (such as Apple's popular iPod) and listen on the go!

How to get your free audio book digital download:

1. Visit www.tatepublishing.com and click on the elLIVE logo on the home page.
2. Enter the following coupon code:
   1ae1-9daa-8178-7a74-2185-372d-ef2a-6aba
3. Download the audio book from your elLIVE digital locker and begin enjoying your new digital entertainment package today!

CPSIA information can be obtained
at www.ICGtesting.com
Printed in the USA
LVOW02s2315201016
509641LV00003B/8/P